The Birdhouse, Or

# THE BIRDHOUSE,

# OR

POEMS BY

JAMIE DOPP

Ekstasis Editions

National Library of Canada Cataloguing in Publication Data

Dopp, Jamie
  The birdhouse, or


  Poems.
  ISBN 1-894800-11-7

  I. Title.
PS8557.O63B57 2002      C811'.54      C2002-910741-5
PR9199.3.D5565B57 2002

Acknowledgements:
Poems from this collection have appeared in *Canadian Literature*,
*The New Quarterly*, and *Event*.


Published in 2002 by:
Ekstasis Editions Canada Ltd.
Box 8474, Main Postal Outlet            Ekstasis Editions
Victoria, B.C. V8W 3S1                          Box 571
                                     Banff, Alberta ToL oCo

THE CANADA COUNCIL | LE CONSEIL DES ARTS
FOR THE ARTS | DU CANADA
SINCE 1957 | DEPUIS 1957

BRITISH
COLUMBIA
ARTS COUNCIL
Supported by the Province of British Columbia

*The Birdhouse, Or* has been published with the assistance of grants
from the Canada Council for the Arts and the Cultural Services
Branch of British Columbia.

FOR WENDY
AND THE BIRDHOUSE BOYS

# Contents

*Teaching Dreams*

*Arse Poetica*

# THUMBING IT

*for Misao, who worried about it*

Try it and I'll try to make room for you.
I'll pull over, sweep the junk off
the other seat, turn over a peace sign
and pop the lock. I'll ask where you're headed
and when you say *there*, I'll say *great, so am I*
even if, strictly speaking, this isn't true.

I know how it is. That lifetime at the side
of the road, the clamp-jawed cars,
trying to assume the right posture
(part orphan, part don't-fuck-with-me),
licking your thumb now and then
for good luck or no reason or just to feel

the shucked air. And if someone stops
—well, then you worry about the crazies.
You glance in the open door (whiff of—what?
sound of—what?) and remember the one
who passed transports over the double line,
who rolled joints with two hands

at ninety miles an hour while steering
with his knee. You live in dread
of the lesser and greater dangers,
the droners, the ones who wall you in
with *me, me, me*, or the ones waiting
to write on your body with a knife.

Try it and I will not be one of those.
Try it and I'll try to see at least one thing
through your eyes. I'll offer you a seat,
make a little small talk (*nice not
to travel alone, eh?*) then leave you
to yourself. After a while

I'll get tired (it's a long way, after all)
and ask if you want to drive. If you do,
we'll trade seats. I'll offer a tip or two
(it's still my car, it's got my personality
—or is that an illusion?) then curl up
and close my eyes. Now you have the wheel,

you make your own sense of the solid
and broken lines. You drive on until
there is, inevitably, a fork—will you go
this way or that? Maybe you steal
a glance back at me, try to read
the intention on my face, but by then

I'm just the question mark
dreaming in the seat beside you.

# THE BIRDHOUSE,

# OR

# The Birdhouse, Or

HE ATTEMPTS TO INTRODUCE HIS SONS TO THE
USES OF CERTAIN TOOLS, AND IS STRUCK BY A
NUMBER OF OBSERVATIONS ABOUT FATHERHOOD,
WITH THREE MINOR MIRACLES AND AN EXTENDED
DISCOURSE ON A SIGNIFICANT BUT RARELY
CONSIDERED PART OF THE HUMAN BODY.

1. Passing the Salt

How it happens.

There is the sweet smell
of amniotic fluid,
the placenta, dying, yet to descend,
you have the scissors in your hand
            (surgical gloves)
        and someone passes you
the blood-slick blue cord.

Then you are mopping up your plate
and Benjamin says
            "I know, Dad! Why don't we
            build a birdhouse?"

You hesitate a moment
before replying
            "A lovely idea, Benjamin.
            Right after dinner.
            And, of course, I'll need
            lots of help from you."

13

The implication
being
  "Father and son."
being
  "A chance to gain
  some knowledge of tools."

As usual, you begin with certain
lies, the confidence
of the well-practiced father, the tall
teller.

For one thing, we never
keep the saltshaker on the table.

For another, the implications are
matters of desire.

What really caused
that moment of hesitation?

      Earlier that day, Benjamin and I went to the hardware store
to pick up a few things. While
      we were there, he noticed a birdfeeder, one of those
plexiglass things you fill with seed and
      hang from a branch. Seventeen bucks. Until that moment he
had never had an interest in
      birdfeeders. Now, he wanted this one. Now, life was not
worth living without this exact
      one. He tried logic, he tried pleading, he tried whining. Then
he threw a fit. He kicked me
      and screamed at the top of his lungs, and when I tried to
comfort him, he beat me around the
      head with his open hands. Blood rushed to my temples. I
said (confusing one object for
      another): "Oh Benjamin, we could make a much nicer
birdhouse ourselves."

How could I say no?

3. RED MEAT

There are also errors of omission.

At the hospital, for instance, where is
the body of the mother?

There is also the fact that we have not one
but two sons.
Our second, Stephen, was at the table that night as well.
His dinner was half-eaten and half
on the floor.
Any account of the birdhouse that does not show this
is hopelessly lacking.

The truth is I did not actually
"cut the cord" at Benjamin's birth,
I only "trimmed" what was left
after the nurse had done her work.

The truth is only with Stephen
was I father enough
        (the well-practiced)
to make that first cut.

There is also the fact that dinner
was a chicken stirfry, a request of mine,
and that the food was prepared
by Wendy.
That afternoon, while Stephen napped
and Benjamin and I
fought over a seventeen dollar birdfeeder,
Wendy chopped vegetables, some of which she had picked
from our garden. As is her habit,
she diced the chicken breasts
with a pair of scissors.

This is part of the birdhouse too.
Just as is the fact that
while the boys and I selected wood downstairs
Wendy finished clearing the table,
and that somewhere between
the first and third version of the roof
she finished stacking the washed dishes
in the tray.

Which reminds me that "cutting the cord"
is an awful lot like
the father cutting the Thanksgiving turkey,
as if, after all that labour, the woman
must relinquish her claim,
as if the knife
        (the scissors)
                after so many incisions
is too dangerous for a woman to wield.

Which reminds me that the poem is
                (always)
        in danger of becoming
like those refrigerated packages at Safeway,
styrofoam backing and transparent stretch-wrap
under fluorescent lights,
the unviolent bloodless nourishment
        (the bolt, the hook, the knife)
we raise on our forks each night.

4. The Birdhouse, or The Somewhat Seamless Narrative
   of What Happened Next


After dinner we went down to where
the tools waited, laid out in their
metal coffins or hung like
weapons on the wall. We collected
scraps of wood and elbowed paint
cans out of the way, and though I
had never made a birdhouse before
it didn't matter. As usual, the boys
wanted to help. As usual, "help"
involved the threat of chaos. Stephen
took it as his job to leave
bite marks on my calf. Benjamin
tried the saw but only managed
to hack skin from the back of
his hand, so I cut a piece
of wood for him, fixed it in
the vice and tried to demonstrate
how to use a file, at which point he
screamed "I know!" and grabbed
the file from me, took his own
two swipes at the splintered edge,
tossed it to the floor and
said: "You do it, Dad."

            As usual
I was struck by the contradictions
of love, my desire and the casualness
of my anger, the way it appeared
at a toss to become part
of the story. Like the way
Benjamin, in an act with all
the outward form of generosity,
gave Stephen his own block
of wood, a rough-cut two-by-four,

and Stephen ran off with it
toward the stairs, a spike in
the wood pressed hard against
the balloon of his stomach. The
ambiguity of that. The absolute
imperative. And, as usual,
the birdhouse became as much for me
as them, an assertion of something
about order or art, so much so
that I did the roof over three
times before getting it right.
When the birdhouse was done, I
held it at arm's length and was
and was not surprised. As usual,
we had survived the spike and
my irritation and an almost full
can of paint that had somehow
toppled from the bench (the metal
edge biting concrete inches
from our toes), and not only that,
but the birdhouse actually looked
like a birdhouse. When they
saw it, my sons began to dance
and sing, and Benjamin paused
only long enough to shout:
"Let's get the ladder now
and hang it in the tree!"

5. LIKE THE BIRDHOUSE ITSELF, THE NARRATIVE IS ONLY SEAMLESS
   FROM A DISTANCE


Not that it is necessarily a lie.
There is the father's tendency
to be taller, I admit that.
There is the usual failure to digress.
The problem with "lie" however
is that it implies "truth"
elsewhere.
No
          (not "here" either).

Just that the seamless narrative
doesn't  (can't)
show you that to care for children
is to experience
      you start a project but
      you grab a book and
      pour a coffee but
          (it's cold)
      and a thought
      you start
      but

nor does it tell you that at a crucial moment
I gave myself a blood blister, and the blister
reminded me of a leech,
which reminded me briefly of my father
        (all those summers burning leeches
        off our bodies around a fire),
and, now, thinking of "father"
makes me wonder:

that a baby in the womb is a parasite
that a suckling child can draw blood
that some days my arms feel punctured by the carrying
that the night cries invade our dreams
that sometimes I say I "draw strength" from my family
that conception is not a selfless act
that a "wanted" child is one you have for yourself

and this leads me
        to consider
that leech, the writer.

You could say there
is something symbiotic
        (parent and child)
        (father and son)
        (writer and . . . )
                and if you did
I would have to reply
that, yes, this is one version

the version

in which I need not look up
as Stephen breaks for the stairs,
the spike pricking his navel
        (the pliers closing on my thumb).

My getting from the workbench to him
is not part of that story
        (one step and another
        the terror in between
        the instinctive over-riding
        of terror)

not snatching the two-by-four

not yelling at Benjamin
    (the hurt on his face)

not taking Stephen in my arms
    (his outrage, his flailing)

not my fatherly calm words
apologies, explanations

not my thumb
    (the scream of sheered vessels
      contradicting every word I say)

## 6. A Digression on Navels

*

There are innies and outies.

*

Consider the yin and yang of navels, the dialectic of.

An innie is like the dent a bullet makes on a road sign.
An outie is like the dent a bullet makes on a road sign.

*

For most people, there is a gradual evolution from one to the other. We begin with an extreme outie, which is cut with surgical scissors and pinched off with a pin. Anything outside the pin turns black and falls off, leaving a large pink knob. Over time, this knob appears to shrink, though really it is an effect of the body growing around it. With the development of the abdominal muscles, the outie is encircled, overtaken, sunk.

An exception is pregnant women. At a certain point in the growth of the baby, the woman's navel pops back out. Sometimes, to the embarrassment of the woman, the navel becomes so pronounced as to show through two or three layers of clothing. In our family, this condition is known as "projectile belly-button."

Perhaps "projectile belly-button" is in fact a kind of sympathetic magic, a symbolic reversal of what the evolution from outie to innie seems to signify: the gradual loss of our connection to our mothers.

*

There are, of course, sexual implications. Which immediately raises the issue of sexual politics. *You fit into me like an outie into an innie.*

Imagine if people took the sexual symbolism of navels seriously. Measured by the usual criterion (mine is bigger than yours), the people with the most power, in descending order, would be: a newborn baby, a child, a woman with "projectile belly-button." Men, on the other hand, would be reduced to glancing at one another in the shower and noticing all those innies. Each man defined by an absence, a something missing, a lack that signalled his ultimate dependency on the mother, a hole that meant he could never be whole.

\*

Not to mention hygiene. Think of the ambiguity in the phrase "Make sure to wash yourself down there." If you don't wash out your navel, what happens? You develop belly-button lint.

In polite company it is okay, under certain circumstances, to talk about navels. You can even call them "belly-buttons" if you want. But it is never okay to talk about belly-button lint. If you talk about belly-button lint you are just being gross. Just as it is gross to talk about certain other excretions of the body: ear wax, finger nail caviar, toe jam.

Like those other excretions, belly-button lint is ambiguous. It is of the body and not of the body. A mix of what comes out of us and what we rub up against. A mark of our innie / outie status with the world.

*

Benjamin, I should tell you, once had a special relationship with his. When he was very small, he would comfort himself by cupping it with his hand. It became very comical when, for instance, he was learning how to walk. There he'd be, lurching like a little Frankenstein, and if he seemed about to fall he'd try at the same time to balance himself and to grab himself *down there.*

Unfortunately, what allowed Benjamin such a good grip on his navel (its pronounced outie-ness), was ultimately diagnosed as the result of a hernia. A condition in which the muscles allow what should remain inside the body out. Our G.P. said that we had a choice: surgery now when Benjamin was small and unlikely to remember it, or surgery later when it was sure to be a trauma.

In a way, it is fitting that a navel should drive home the vulnerability of Benjamin's body to me. That trace of a totally dependant, though totally cared for, time. Of course I understood about vulnerability before, rationally, but reason could not prepare me for that moment in the entrance to the operating room, Benjamin mildly sedated in my arms, and the nurse comes out the door in her green gown, mask dangling from her neck . . . and takes him from me.

Afterwards, he wouldn't take anything for the pain. He'd just suck on a popsicle for a while, then doze back off to sleep. We got him home, a couple of hours after the surgery, and he and I sat in the rocking chair, him curled up in a blanket, me soothing both of us by a gentle rocking.

At one point, he woke up long enough to eat two popsicles in a row and then immediately threw them up again. A cool pink-orange liquid drenched me from shoulders to knees. Then he was asleep again. I didn't get up. I stayed for about an hour that way, drenched and rocking, Benjamin asleep under his miraculously dry blanket. I must admit I took a certain gratification in it. It seemed right, somehow, that I should have to sit there like that, a payback for my role as a father: that in helping to give life I would also, inevitably, give pain.

Before the operation, Benjamin's belly-button looked like one of those bullet-headed Fisher Price people. Afterwards, what was left of it looked like the tied end of a pink balloon.

＊

Stephen, typically, has his own take on them. No doubt this comes from his experience as the second child. The child who must define himself against, who arrives on the scene to find someone else already at the centre of affection, who is the supplement, who is required (despite the parents' best intentions) to battle for his share of love.

For whatever reason, Stephen has so far shown an uncanny knack for finding the sensitive points on the body. Adam's apple, breasts, back of the thighs, penis, vagina, belly-button. Every once in a while, back when he was still nursing, I'd hear Wendy let out a shriek. I'd rush to the sound, leaving Benjamin alone with his toys (a fact perhaps not unnoticed by the baby) and find her holding Stephen at arm's length. "No biting!" she'd shout. "No biting!" And he'd give her a delighted, devilish, two-tooth grin.

Stephen understands that if he pokes in the right place his father will jump to attention. The belly-button is a favourite target. For one thing, I tend to protect myself elsewhere first. This is because of what happened one day when we were wrestling. Benjamin came in high and I put both hands up to catch him, and in the same instant Stephen came in low, burying his face in my pyjama bottoms and chomping *down there*.

In this context, Stephen's act on the night of the birdhouse was a masterful tactic, a brilliant reversal: poke himself instead of me. As I took off after him, I could see he had that devilish grin on his face, which leads me to suspect he had just learned an important lesson: that sensitive points are as much emotional as physical. As I reached my hands out for the block of wood, I could almost hear him thinking, "There's more than one way to the centre of the story."

29

There is the inertia of words.

When I say "father"
when I say "son"
when I say "the body of the mother"

the way a pushed swing
will slow
    (a pendulum tending)
to the vertical.

For example, I didn't have
a blueprint for a birdhouse
yet I built one that looked like
"a blueprint for a birdhouse."

And when Benjamin said "Let's get the ladder"
I didn't have a blueprint for what to do next
but I understood that birdhouses were for hanging
and that ladders were for hanging

and for this reason
though a part of me was thinking
"fuck father and son"
"fuck knowledge of tools"

I went to get the ladder.

> In our front yard, there is a tall pine tree, trimmed up to the
> height of the house. From the first set of remaining branches
> hang two swings, one for Stephen and one for Benjamin.
> Between these swings, on a third branch protruding at right
> angles, I hung the birdhouse.

Before I went up the ladder with it, Wendy (who had come out by this point) took a felt marker and wrote on the side:

*June 10, 1996*
*By Benjamin, Jamie.*

I attached it with eye-screws and binder twine. Wendy gave me the lengths of twine, a little prickly to the touch, which she unwound from a ball and cut with scissors.

Afterwards, Benjamin wanted to try the ladder.
Ladders, he told me, are for climbing.
While I stood below him
holding the aluminum sides,
I thought again of my own father,
how ladders always remind me of him,
the years he spent washing one window or another.
I thought of the first time I worked with him
when he showed me how to carry a ladder
like a twenty-four foot rifle
on my shoulder.

And then, for some reason, I remembered
Benjamin's first joke.
It was earlier that week,
he was on his swing
(back and forth)
and I was trying to get him to pump
(the inertia of "underduck")
when suddenly, at the top of his lungs, he shouted:
"Milk is for eating and food is for drinking!"

That night, I had two nightmares.

In the first, I am on the roof of our house. I am near the peak, holding on with one hand and fixing shingles with the other. My ladder is a few feet away, angling the long way down to the ground. After a while, I glance over and Benjamin is there. He has climbed the ladder and is now stepping onto the roof. I tell him "No!" but he does not listen. Then I can see fear on his face. He reaches out to me. I want to reach back but I have one hand full of tools and the other holding onto the roof. He falls.

In the second, I am looking to rent a room. I arrive at a boarding house, like a place I lived in as a student years ago. Someone shows me around. I wonder if I should take the room. My wondering reminds me of the reason for my move: I have broken up with Wendy. Then I remember that we have children and that I am about to begin living by myself. Loneliness.

The title of this section is an example of:
>a) the leech poet at work,
>b) the poem as red meat,
>c) another gratuitous reference to blood.

There is never
>ONE REASON PERIOD
>>for not making love

or for making a birdhouse,
not one reason for a dream
or a poem
or the gift of a block of wood.

Like the place of the social order
in Benjamin's joke
                    (celebration)
                            anxiety
                                    (freedom from)
                                            mastery of.

Which shows that repetition does not necessarily
make things clearer.
                    (See "blood").

What caused the dreams?

What happens when the poem really avoids
the meat aisle at Safeway?

## 9. The Coming of the Birds, or A Somewhat Romantic View of the Next Morning

After the ladder is away and the children asleep
and there is silence but for the soft breath beside you;
after the hour you lay awake before falling
into a dream of falling
when you realize that the birdhouse
was another of your attempts at passing for a father,
a repetition of "father"
and the word "passing" makes you think of
the salt taste of blood;
after you are prodded to attention by Stephen's night cry
and come back to bed at 3:15
to find the woman you love, back turned, clutching a pillow
like a refugee asleep on a bag of flour,
and you realize how the words "mother" and "father"
have invaded your dreams, your making of love,
how even when you admit the contradictions to one another,
the way you have been ambushed by emotions
—even then, everything has a way of settling back
into "father" and "mother";
after you doze uneasily in the pre-dawn, dreaming
of loneliness, and there is a sound of wind,
then the sound of small, running feet that goes away
and comes back louder
and finally stops at the foot of the bed,
you open you eyes.
There is Benjamin. He whispers:
"Mom! Dad! The birds have come!"

He leads you to the livingroom window
and sure enough, there are sparrows, a male and a female,
building a nest in the birdhouse.
They fly back and forth, shuttling straw,
and it is miraculous the way
they navigate in and out of the swaying circle of door,
the way they seem to hover in a blur of wings
before entering.
You are so moved that when Stephen cries from his crib
you rush back to get him,
and the four of you creep onto the front porch,
so close
you can hear a soft scratching,
like the sound of a pencil marking a page,
each time the sparrows' feet touch down.

You are surprised and not surprised by the way
these moments come,
the four of you on the porch like that,
the birdhouse not only looking like a birdhouse but actually one.
If someone came walking then
and looked back across your grey fence from the sunlit road,
she would see a family constructed
from the very blueprint of love.

In the end, there is the problem
with "polite company,"
the need to avoid the poem
that practices proper hygiene
*down there.*

So:

What are we to make of that inscription?

How it effaces the mother,
and yet is
      (also)
                the mother's way of
putting her mark on
the birdhouse. As if, after all that labour.

                The ambiguity
of that. Like the twine itself, with its prickled
surface, its corona of fine threads.

Or:

What are we to make of the sparrows?

The wingspeed of
      (mother, father)
the movement in / out of that door
like a navel.

              "Soon," we told Benjamin
                    (and Stephen)
"there will be babies."

The trick is to maintain the connection
between Benjamin and I in the rocking chair
and a birdhouse that swings between swings.

Like not omitting the ambiguity
of dishes, the way
they can be an adult's time alone,
not treasured exactly
                    (the poem always in danger
                    of becoming the father's apology)
                              but perhaps
the lesser of two labours.

Like "scissors."

Which shows that repetition does not necessarily
make a father.

Like Wendy's labours
                    (one, two)
                              after which she had
to take a rhogram shot,
a large needle, the kind where the doctor draws
blood back into the syringe
before pressing down.

How it happens.

The shot required only
if the father is not Rh-negative as well,
and yet
        (how)
                they never
tested me.

Why?

"No point in taking chances," explained the nurse.
"After all, you can never really
be sure of the father."

The ambiguity
of "that."

# LIMES

## LIMES

Sometimes you go to the store
and it's dusk, say, one of those premature
December nights, four-thirty, and your lover not home yet
from work. There is the contrast
between the washed out look of the street
and the fruits in the window, avocados, bananas,
oranges, lemons, track-lit and arranged
on green matting.
Inside you joke, as usual, about work, about
how long the day seems,
and the husband, as usual, throws up his hands.
"I'm up at 4AM for the market. I get everything
fresh for the day. Thirty years from Italy I'm up at 4AM
and what have I got?" For the third time that week
he asks if you want to buy the store,
you laugh and ask how much and he says:
"How much you got in your pockets?"

Perhaps the wife laughs too.
Sometimes she is at the cash-register, or towelling
the floors. Sometimes she crows about the daughter
who married well. The wedding cost
twelve thousand dollars, it almost put them
in the poorhouse, it was so beautiful.
The day she tells you this
you imagine her dancing with the father of the groom,
corsage, seamed stockings, skirt square
about her hips. Then the husband
slams down his clipboard: "A doctor!
How much you think a doctor makes?
And every week for free food they still
come to papa."

41

Meanwhile, you have worked your way down the aisle
and back. What you have really come in for
are lemons, to finish
a recipe, something to go with candles, wine,
apologies (your lover
on the subway somewhere, hanging by one arm,
refusing eye contact). You decide you need
something different.
Beside the lemons in the window
are smaller green fruits
the shape of testicles.

## 2. GRINGA

One morning I confused salt for sugar,
spread my toast white
and crushed the loaded wafer to my tongue.
For days after I could not get the sea-taste
from my mouth. I drank
lime-aid, glass after glass, the limes
pulled down from the tree out back, squeezed
and carefully sugared.

This was in Tehuacán, the place of my first love.
She was American, auburn hair and green, green
eyes. I remember the taste
of her eyes, the back seat of a car near the plaza mayor,
evening's rise, the last accidental notes
of a mariachi band.
The first time we kissed
I raced down empty streets and sent signs
swinging, played soccer with rocks, candy wrappers, cans,
and arrived at my boarding house
without a key. Then, something
forbidden, I climbed the bars over a window, heel-toed
across the gravel roof
and swung myself inside by a branch
of the lime tree. To my joy, there
was Señor Paredes, heels planted, face
squeezed with anger.

Our final Sunday, we met at the cafe Peñafel, drank beer
with lemon and salt.
Later, in the tropical back seat, we kissed
until our chins were juiced, our cheeks aching, and she
lowered her face onto my chest.
I put my arms around her shoulders, heartbeat
in my mouth,
and remembered strolling the square that afternoon,
what a radiant couple we had made,
and imagined the romantic figure I would cut
as the separated lover.
After a while she began to sob.
I said, "I will never forget you"
and meant it.
I remember how she looked up at me then,
the bitterness of foreknowledge,
the taste of those green eyes.

### 3. THE WORD "BOURGEOIS"

The taste, like tonic water, hence
the applicability to gin.
Unlike the lemon, which is clear and tart, a flavour
that leaves your mouth feeling like a washed window,
the lime is more ambiguous, murky; it tastes
of rind.

In the mornings they were like the shells of old
golf-balls, on end-tables, in glasses, in
the sink. Floating in the remains
of dead ice-cubes.
How I hated them! I would pick them up
like something from the bottom of a pond, evidence
of corruption.

In the mornings I saw the rind of lives, shavings
from the lathe of decades,
the bitten pulp, the bitter skins curled
like the fingers of the dying.
The one with cigarette lines giving her a
bullet hole mouth.
The one with gut hairs spiking between buttons.
The one whose wife left seven years ago,
still spitting her name nightly like a seed.

This was the year I learned the word "bourgeois,"
how it could sabotage talk
of boats, private schools, vacations in Cancun.
The year my mother's best friend got drunk, started
bawling (salt drops
in her Tom Collins), demanded to know
why I hated her.

Also the year I took up horseshoes, the clear, breakfast-bell
ring of them.
In the mornings I'd hold one in each fist to clang away
the sand, until my mother leaned out
to complain of a singing
head. I had
the vocabulary, I had just thrown two ringers in a row.
Still, I did not get it
when she said:
"Something didn't agree with me last night.
I think it was the limes."

4. TRACE OF AN ACCENT

When the connections seem clear, the lime is left out
in the sun, juice turns
to air, seeds to bone, skin
begins the long retreat back to powder.
You play within new boundaries, in bounds and out, centre
line, goal keeper's box,
and at half-time gulp Gatoraid, sugared green water
in big mouthed bottles.

An away game. You have scored
your only goal ever, and at half-time
clack down unfamiliar hallways
in your cleats. In one there is Becky,
the girl you dreamed about last year but were afraid
to talk to (she now attends
this strange school), and she recognizes you, asks
what the score of the game is and who
scored the goal.

Sometimes it happens that way.
Other times you lose
your temper, twist divots from the field, curse down
your own star player.
His name is Johnnie Byrne, and he
is a prima dona (though aren't
you all): flashy red hair and the trace
of an accent. You spit out
a name you know will hurt though you are not sure
of its origin, and he unexpectedly
bows his head.

You think you have won something then,
though you are not sure what
or if you like it, until the next game, at home,
the two of you powdering the lines,
when he wheels
and claps a blinding handful of white powder
over your eyes:
"You want limey I'll give you limey
you fucking Canuck."

5. LUNCH AT THE DEMITASSE CAFÉ

How it happens. You see
those smaller green fruits and think
"lie down with me," or "lie me
down," something like that,
you think about Tom Collins and (inevitably) politics.
Then things begin
to mutate, you follow lines you did not expect, a region
of hidden grudges, unexpected
ambiguous victories, you tell your lover
and she says "if you really want to talk
about the relationship between fruit and testicles—
think kiwis."

And she's right. You can imagine one, now, cupped
in two fingers, the weight
of it, the way you feel yourself in the shower.
You get philosophical, think life
is like that,
all those times you headed out for lemons
and ended up with
something else, or those other times
you headed out without a recipe, said to yourself
"Live random!" and ended up with
the same old boring fruit.

Like the kiwis. Part of you hates her
for saying that, the way it squeezes life from
your carefully picked words,
but part of you
loves her too, again, all those delicious new
possibilities.
For example, the fine fuzz on a kiwi.
What do you make of that?

To celebrate, you go out for lunch together,
find yourself in front of, say, a steaming
croissant, brie, grapes, half moon of orange,
and to finish the arrangement
two perfect round wafers
of kiwi. Before you
dig in, you sit back to admire it all,
the faint odour of sex in the warm brie,
your lover's voice,
the colours white, gold, violet, orange
and the inside of the kiwis—a perfect
lime green.
Oh, how hungry it makes you.

# ED'S RED CAR

# ED'S RED CAR

Has a black dashboard split open
by the sun. The driver's side window
is sealed shut with duct tape,
red, as it turns out, a lucky
match (it's what I had on hand).
More tape covers the holes where

the rear reflectors used to be.
The engine on Ed's red car starts
hot or cold but not in between.
It also has a leaky gasket
(when you open the hood you can see
the mess, a black skin creeping

down the engine block). When I asked
the guy at the garage if it was
worth fixing, he took a step back,
squinted his eyes and said:
"Just remember. Oil is cheap."
There are two kid seats in

Ed's red car. Generally a shoe
or two. Crushed bread stick. Sometimes
a dead sea creature in a plastic pail.
The paint job is pretty well gone,
it has that bleached out look
old cars get in climates where

things don't rust. But how the car
shines when we wash it, when I roll it
through the gate onto our front lawn
and Benjamin soaps the wheels
and Stephen lurches unsteadily
with the hose. We washed it like this

the day before Ed died. I remember
hoping he could see us, propped up
on his porch across the street.
Probably not. He was on extra morphine then
and in and out of consciousness.
Even so I cheered on the boys

and we worked our rags until the car
gleamed in the July sun, Ed's
red car, its creaks and smells
and impervious stubborn mystery,
radiant as a human body
viewed in the light of love.

# TRAFFIC

On our street we are rather stupid
about emotion. Oh we care for one
another, sure, but you have to learn
to read the signs. Like the way

ladders get passed around. Michael
borrowed ours to stain his house
and returned it freckled as
my back. We used Ron and Laura's

to install our new window (we needed
two). The children, of course,
swap toys. Benjamin and Christie
traded a digger for a dump truck

and Clarke and Stephen sometimes deal
in miniature cars. Now and then
Nigel exchanges his wagon for a
thank you and please. Many things

are never meant to be returned: Michael's
telephone and third bicycle and
yard sale treasures, the plants from
Marilyn and Dave, the book Evangeline

gave Benjamin (it was hers when she
was a baby). Sometimes I wish
we could just say it in words, say
"friend," say "neighbour," that we

didn't have to traffic like this
in things, but I also know that words
can be an easy out, who better
to know this than a poet, all

those poems like unfaithful lovers
whispering "I love you." The fruit dish
we gave Susan was really a kiss.
I buckle myself into Ed's red car
and feel his arms around me.

# THE NEW HOUSE

Predictably, the new house is
large. Not vulgar, exactly, but
lacking character—a big, beige,
suburban box on a street of
old working class homes without
a right angle left in them.
The developer, whom we know as
Dave, wears nerdy glasses and
drives a black pickup truck. Not
a bad guy, I don't blame him for
trying to make a buck, though
it was hard to watch the
excavator roll like a tank
over Ed's berries. When fallers came
to take down the Gary oak, Dave
sat with us on the curb. There was
something sad and beautiful
about it, the fallers swinging
from branch to branch on their
safety lines, chainsaws dangling
from their belts, the way they
took down the larger limbs in
sections and dropped the pieces, one
by one, until there was a pile
like children's blocks.
"Look at that," said Dave. "The thing
was diseased. Probably would have
fallen anyway." During the construction,
he was there once a day, spreading
blueprints on his tailgate,
dropping off smaller supplies, smoking
with the workers. Now and then
he'd smile at us and, in an
emotional, almost sentimental

voice, say what a special home
it was going to be for someone.
A year later, the house still
'unsold, he'd lost some of his swagger.
We gave him advice, how to
tidy the yard, how to spruce up
the garden, all the while
trying not to look smug.
He shrugged. Who could've
known the market would go soft?
In the spring, daffodils
and grape hyacinths pushed up
through the new sod,
and Dave confided to my
neighbour that he thought the
place was jinxed. Before the
latest open house, he
came by with a lawnmower
in his truck. I watched him
take it down, prime
the engine, pull the cord.
Then he was striding back and
forth over the green grass,
sunlight flaring off his spectacles,
nonchalance or grim determination
on his face. Now and then,
chewed up bits of flower,
yellow or blue, came coughing
out of the machine. And
after a while, as shredded
petals swirled like butterflies
around him, Dave's lips
began to move. He was
either singing or muttering
something like "Fucking garden,
fucking garden."

# The Garden

Not an original strategy, his
keeping busy to keep death
at bay. I see it
in my grandmother, devoted to family
and the church, and in my workaholic
colleagues, with their conferences

and committees and e-mails from
worried editors. Still,
there was something special about
Ed's garden, the way the berries
grew so dense you'd have to hack
a trail to pick them, the way

the fruit trees sagged in that
slightly vulgar way of overladen
fruit trees, and the flowers—
so massed and gaudy they seemed
like decorations at
a twenty thousand dollar wedding.

Maybe it was because
I knew the history, how he bought
the extra lot for Nellie, who pined
for another garden,
and because the neighbourhood kids
would climb the Gary oak and look

in his kitchen window; how he
brought in a dozen loads of top soil
and built a white picket fence.
After Nellie died, he took out nothing
she had planted, only added more
and more again, especially berries,

so that we used to see him
picking for days on end, in a canvas hat
against the blazing sun, a plastic container
on a string around his neck. He was
the kind of man who made
thirty gallon vats of wine even though

he rarely drank. Not long after he
knew he was dying, he bought two
truckloads of manure and unloaded them
himself. Would you call this
heroic or pathetic or something else?
Myself, I can't say. I only know

I used to be ironic about my grandmother,
my colleagues, the way they seemed
to be trying to make themselves indispensable
(my grandmother, half-blind and past eighty,
on a church visit to comfort
"the old people") until I realized

busyness like that is not about
claiming special value, or even expertise, but
only about creating the illusion that
something in this world requires
your attention—that something, against
all logic and appearances, is

incomplete. Even now, I imagine
Ed haunting the white house
that is no longer his, up in the night
with a glass of water worrying about
the berries—how they'll be rotting on the cane
if they're not picked soon. I imagine him

human, his old bones, the gnarled hands
that shake whenever he turns a bolt or
drinks a glass of water but that
always get on with the job.
Never happier than when heartsick
over things undone.

## DEATH DOESN'T CHANGE ANYONE

My friend's father is dying.
He phones me up, sometimes late at night,
to whisper his grief.
Because we are who we are,
men more comfortable with emotion than our fathers
but still skittish about tears,
we usually circle around the topic for awhile,
work our way towards it through
anecdotes about childhood, our jobs
and kids, our current bumbling
into middle-age.

The dying, I know, has been terrible
and slow, three years
of cancer hollowing out his father's bones,
so that the family has had to watch
the pitiless decay of this large man who worked
all his life with his hands,
a man who took up space equally
with body and opinions, until all that remained was
wasted arms needing help to raise
a cigarette.
Two weeks ago the old man took to the couch,
stubborn with pain,
and today he waits, pinioned by the usual needles and tubes,
in the terminal ward at Jubilee.

One night my friend says,
"I wish we could talk.
More than anything else, what I want
is a few moments with him, a few seconds, even,
when we really talk, not even to say anything directly about love

—God knows, it would be enough
if we could just forgive each other
what we have to forgive."

When he tells me this, I remember
my friends who have died slow cancer deaths—
Michele, Jan, Larry, Skeeter, Ed—
how their dying was shaped by who they were and nothing else,
how the ones who fought in life fought,
who cursed cursed, laughed laughed, talked talked,
how each fought and cursed and laughed and talked
in his or her own measure
and his or her own way.
Afterwards, I could never remember a moment
of revelation, no moment when a friend became incandescent
or uncannily wise,
no moment when someone became
something new . . . none of that.
And afterwards, after the fear and sadness, I was also
much the same, no great new insights,
just my usual pipe dreams and virtues and neuroses
tempered only by a deepened humility
before the wonder and fragility of life.

Tonight, my friend has been crying, is
crying—he doesn't try
to hide it.
I expect him to tell me
it's over, his father is dead, but instead he says,
"I went to see him again.
I decided, finally, we'd talk.
So I get to his room, he's lying there,
I say, 'Hi Dad'—and before I can say anything else
he says, 'What'd you pay for parking?'
Just like that: 'What'd you pay for parking?'

So I tell him . . . and the next thing
we start to argue,
he tells me I've always been stupid with money,
I lose my temper too,
I tell him, I tell him . . ."

The house is dark.
I am in my housecoat on the kitchen floor,
my lover, my children asleep
behind closed doors.
I hold the receiver and imagine that somewhere
lights are shining.
"We are such idiots," my friend whispers.
"He could be dead tomorrow
and all we do tonight is argue
the price of parking."

# TEACHING
# DREAMS

## ELECTION NIGHT

*May 30, 1996.*
*Victoria, B. C.*


So I'm at the "victory" party except
it's not at all, not yet,
and the TV announcers are going on
about how the uncertainty could go on.
I've had two beers, or
been had by two beers (if you know what I mean),
and everyone else around me, as usual,
seems to have it more together,
as if they grew up
in a family that knew Tommy Douglas personally,
and this was nothing
compared to Saskatchewan in '46.
So I'm at that crossroads,
where either I dip into the cooler again
and figure on a taxi home
and a particular grumpiness in the morning,
or I make
a break for it.

The car, well, let me tell you,
it's my friend Ed's,
in other words it belongs to the uncle
of Bob Williams, cabinet minister and crony
of Dave Barrett, who no doubt
knows lots of people
who knew Tommy Douglas personally,
so, as I turn the key,
I feel a bit like a party disloyalist
but what the hell.

It's all worth it, when I crawl into bed with Wendy,
and we do spoons.
Benjamin and Stephen are
asleep down the hall (I've kissed them both already).
It's like all those times she's taken my hand
in shopping malls
just before the green scales appear on my neck.
Like the way she'll give me something
to carry in my pocket,
a stone from the beach at Barachois,
one of Stephen's socks, to remind me,
at the worst point of my day out there,
about in here.

Well, as usual, when I'm calm again,
I have this need
to knock on doors, to read aloud, to argue
with the news.
So we turn on the radio, softly.

Next thing I've thrown off the covers
and I'm running naked into the livingroom.
I need the confirmation
of graphics, of
talking heads as well as talking.
There in front of the TV
I start bouncing from foot to foot,
partly because
I'm excited, partly because
I'm still naked, then streak back
and drag Wendy from under her warm covers
to do a silly dance.
I grab my dirty underwear from the floor
and shout: "I have to go back to the party!"

So, for the historical record, let me state
I was there.
I was there to shake hands
with the candidate, the other workers, all
those dry palms with their traces
of other lives,
there for Glen Clark on TV, flanked by his family,
speaking of hope
and the future.

Afterwards, I pull back into our driveway
and take a long hard look at our NDP sign.
From the time between
my second departure and second return, someone,
a person with no other connection
to my life, has spray-painted
a large black "X" through it.
On this night, above all others,
I can appreciate
the ambiguity of the gesture.

## WALKING WITH THE CANDIDATE

In those shoes, yeah.
The ones with the thick rubber soles.
A necessity for:
    1) Stumping.
    2) To ground against
       electric currents.

Easy, right?
Put on a suit,
stick your mouth in front of a mike,
produce opinions and collect:
    1) A big fat cheque.
    2) A bigger, fatter pension.

Anybody
with opinions
can do it.

Yeah, yeah. Except for:
    1) Those electric currents.

Poets, of all people, should understand.
Remember that joke about
the writer and the brain surgeon?
The surgeon says:
    "When I retire I'm going
      to become a writer."
and the writer replies:
    "What a coincidence.
     When I retire I'm going
     to become a brain surgeon."

Believe me when I tell you
I have seen
the scorch marks on the ground.

# To a Young Activist

*for Sarah*

This is for your first campaign
when the candidate you worked for day and night
finished dead last

This is for the half-victories
the paradoxes and contradictions

your shy sister going with you
to Take Back The Night
your father leaving the Against Corporate Rule poster
you taped to the fridge

This is for your mother
her silences that might be pride and might be horror
those times she looks at you
as if she can't believe you grew inside her body

like the time you got your nose pierced
and your mother cried "Gross!"
then listened carefully to your explanation
so she could brag about you later
at the church

This is for our differences
yours and mine
and for the things we have in common

your newly claimed adulthood
your feminism shining like a new skin
my middle-aged implication
in the tangle-footed dance of life

This is for the choices we make each day
our shared refusal
to accept that what we can do
doesn't amount to a hill of beans in this world
and leave it at that

and for the times we both think
more of death than politics

This is for the miracle of chance or genetics or history
that you or I or any of us
should walk upright like this

# THE RAT

When things get rough you fall back
on your systems,
the date books and calendars,
the children's schedules taped to the fridge.
You do chores on regular days,
Thrifty-shop on Monday, music lessons mid-week,
and sex on Friday if you're not
completely spent.

Then one day a mouse wriggles from under
the sandbox tarp.
You are on your way somewhere—say,
a meeting you can't postpone.
Soon there are droppings in the basement, like
rolled up insects, garden dirt,
and one night, after you've shimmied under the blankets,
there is Morse code
in the wall.

Maybe you take half-measures—
stab a trowel at the foundation, its spreading
hieroglyphs—
maybe convince yourself it's enough . . .

until one night the mouse is under your bed,
you hear it scratching like
the living dead, and one of you jumps up to ram on
the light.
You gasp into action, throw clothes and boxes around the room,
blame each other and begin to worry
about disease, the children.

In the depths of it, you find a desperate
clarity, repair
the garage door hingeless for six months,
tape flashing in corners, spread traps and poison pellets.
The poison guarantees internal bleeding, conscious
death, but warns that rodents are rarely eliminated
only controlled.

One morning, you find the body,
tiny, grey, a smear of open mouth.
The children are curious,
they've never seen an animal dead in a trap,
the red eyes, red
in the soft fur where the bar snapped to.
Why? they ask.
Why? you say and lead them
to the grave you have prepared for it, a spade's
worth of hole, the very place you leave
your heel print
after a ceremony
rich with platitudes.

# NOT THIS WORKBENCH

But the one that is a blueprint
behind your eyes, its straight edge
like the bar of a fraction
dividing what you see flatfoot
from what you see on your toes—a world
of benevolent cautions, the smell
of solder, rhythmic
chomp of a handsaw, the infallible
arc of an arm working a hammer.

It reminds you of the man
up the street, Mister Bucinski,
the one you called Hook, as if his injury
were simply in the order
of things, the way the world
divides itself into us and them,
the way every story needs a villain.
How he could sense when a ball went
into his yard, the thrill
of jumping the fence as the door jerked open,
always that saw-toothed voice, the threat to call
the police. How you leered as he
left for work in his deflated suit,
that one half-hollow sleeve, the way
he kept his yard immaculate
because it was all he could do.
You remember how you frightened each other
with stories of him, how he would
chase you around the block, the hook
flashing above his head—the shudder
of pleasure as you contemplated that,
the other shudder as you took your turn
knocking at his door.

Today, as you stand here
in your own basement
among tools you inherited and the familiar
insistent questions of your son, it comes to you
like the unexpected quiet when
the furnace cuts out, what it was
you feared and craved, why you loved
to dare from behind the door
that image of a man not whole.

For a moment the hammer loses
its familiar balance, as if the handle
were a crumbling bone, then things become
solid again. You hear
your voice echo a long ago voice
warning of the dangers,
there is the shuffle of impatient feet

and from outside an engine's roar
reminds you of the world
of men, that world you cannot escape
though you thought you could once, by ignoring
your body for your mind, so that
you know, as you
drop to your knees in search
of the fallen nail (the hammer's claw
dangling from the hook
of your fingers) that your son
is now on tiptoes, his delicate fingers reaching
to where the light catches metal.
Against all your warnings, your feeble
attempts to ease the passage,
he will return flatfoot
only to admire
the bloody tattoo on his wrist.

# THE DAY HE TURNED FORTY

A griffin sank its claws
into his back

He spent his party
drugged and drunk and getting drunker
and when the pain was too much
curled up in the "recovery"
position on the lawn
(it was an outdoor party)

And on that day
he was more than usually in love
with his own words
and shook off the griffin long enough
to read from his latest manuscript
(which was much improved
by Tylenol and beer)
until his guests began to smile
in that tentative way
of people looking for an exit

And in the fetal position again
communing with worms
he wondered if the pain was
in fact another kidney stone (god forbid)
at which point his sons came skipping
called him the usual taunting names
and challenged him to wrestle

and for the usual reasons
(love and stupidity
the fact it was his birthday
too much Tylenol and beer)
he said yes

As you would expect
it was *Oedipus Rex* reinterpreted
by the W.W.F.
and he lost six or seven pins in a row
the griffin dug its talons deeper
and he made heroic-idiotic attempts
to blank out the pain

Then his sons
(just like on TV)
put him in "The Pretzel"

There was a
        C R A C K !!!
and he was absolutely and completely
pain free

The day he turned forty
death always seemed on the edge
of his awareness
like sirens on a hot summer night
and he was haunted by
the griffin's master
that slapstick creature in black hood
with bad teeth and bad timing
who comes rapping at the door

but in the end
he brushed himself off
climbed the stairs under his own power
and was amazed to find himself
happy

That night
he spent five full seconds
plucking one white eyebrow hair
then roostered into the bedroom
(where he was pleased to note
he was still married
to the same beautiful young woman)
and announced
"I feel like a million bucks."

## TEACHING DREAMS

Like the one when my first-year class
is Introductory French
and of course I've been faking it
since I don't speak a word
and the students are getting suspicious

Or the one when I forget my lecture notes
and find myself droning banal generalities
before a jury of fifty-five increasingly
in the mood for hanging

Then there are the times I'm late
or can't find the room
in which case I end up rushing
down endless empty corridors
with life sucking radioactive linoleum
and Daliesque clocks
me
   l
     t
     i
      n
     g
from the walls

Sometimes I end up
in regions of the university
I never knew existed
down below somewhere
a subterranean passage warm and bright
and humming with secret machinery

And once by a kind of miracle
I happened upon the right classroom
except there was only one student left by then
a young woman at a front desk writing
in a notebook or journal

I noticed how beautiful she was
and wondered if I should go on with the lesson
(there were officially ten minutes left)
but she took one look at me
gathered her things and made
for the door

As she brushed past
the young woman threw me a sad
and bitter look.
"What do you know
about anything?" she said.

# WHY I ~~LOVED~~ HATED THIS COURSE

Sometimes I found it hard to go to class
because it was so boring

still, the content and instruction
were awesome

The professor asked questions but didn't seem
to want them answered

though I liked how he was extremely flexible
and open to suggestions

It was a great course with excellent readings

which left me wondering if there are
any exciting Canadian texts out there

Lose the beard, okay?

The most stimulating and enjoyable course
I have taken in this department

except that the instructor obviously does not have
the knowledge to explore the topics

The professor raised a number of interesting issues
but we didn't

divulge in them much

Thanks for the thought-provoking questions
with answers so obvious no one answered them

I hate English courses in general
but I do have one piece of advice:

Don't lean against the blackboard
when you lecture

you keep getting chalk dust
on your bum.

*Perhaps the mission of those who love mankind is to make people laugh at the truth, to make truth laugh, because the only truth lies in learning to free ourselves from an insane passion for the truth.*

Umberto Eco, *The Name of the Rose*

*The academy is not paradise. But learning is a place where paradise can be created. The classroom, with all its limitations, remains a location of possibility. In that field of possibility we have the opportunity to labour for freedom, to demand of ourselves and our comrades, an openness of mind and heart that allows us to face reality even as we collectively imagine ways to more beyond boundaries, to transgress. This is education as the practice of freedom.*

bell hooks, *Teaching to Transgress*

So I'm in the middle of the lecture on postmodernism, one of my favourites, a set-piece, when this student rises from her seat. She makes her way to the front of the class and climbs onto my desk. Just like that: not a word, not a smile or a wink, not a glance in my direction. She just climbs up, not six feet from where I'm leaning on the podium, paralyzed by the letter "P" . . . climbs up on the desk and stands there, hands at her sides, tall and fantastic and with an unreadable expression on her face. She looks at the class. The class looks at her.

I don't know what to do, so I do what I always do when I don't know what to do: I keep talking.

I talk until I get to the point where I always mention Umberto Eco, and then there's movement, I can see it reflected in the eyes of the students before me. I steal a glance and the woman is still on the desk, except she is no longer still. Instead she is dancing, slowly, sensuously, her arms rising and falling, her hips working an imaginary hoola-hoop—like a go-go dancer at half-speed. Her eyes are closed now and I feel I should make a comment to her or to the class, something about wouldn't it be nice if we could all hear the music, a comment mildly comical but also gently chiding, respectful but enough to break the spell (because who knows what pressure students are under these days?). But I can't remember her name.

I try to carry on. I talk and talk. I get to the part about Linda Hutcheon and the word "epistemology," and there is a whisper beside me. The whisper grows in my ear until it becomes a song: "I am truth, I am truth, I am troo-oo-oo-ooth."

I talk louder.

Time passes, it must, because I keep on talking (though I'm no longer sure what my point is). I try to recapture the class's attention, try one of my famous anecdotes with the guaranteed guffaw, but the students' eyes are all elsewhere, their eyes are wider than they have ever been for one of my lectures or one of my anecdotes, and in their eyes I can see the woman dancing.

I check again and the woman is still there, still dancing and still singing in a whisper that is now the only thing in the world I can hear, except that now she's naked, absolutely and unabashedly naked, and I think "Oh my God I've got a naked woman in my classroom." Part of me thinks I'm not the kind of poet to have go-go dancing student strippers in my poems but another part of me can't take my eyes off her, just as the students can't take their eyes off her, I want her somehow and am embarrassed by the wanting (I am a happily married man after all). And maybe it's because of her naked-ness or my desire for her or maybe it's just an epiphany born of con-fusion, but I realize all at once that the woman is in fact the woman from my earlier poem, she's the student in my teaching dream when I finally find the classroom who brushes by me and asks what I know. And suddenly I have the deep suspicion that she really is truth, which sets me off in another direction altogether, since I can't decide if there is something sexist in this, a heterosexual man

85

imagining truth as a naked woman, or if this is just my version at this particular moment and everybody else is seeing something else.

At which point she stops.

She breaths, seems to savour the air on her moist skin. She looks at the class, looks at me. Then she throws back her head. And laughs.

She doesn't just laugh, she laughs and laughs and laughs until one by one the students break out into giggles, and soon I am laughing myself even though I can't tell if she is laughing with us or at us or at something that has nothing to do with us. I laugh at my wanton thoughts and my lecture, at Linda Hutcheon and Umberto Eco and the podium I lean on and the letter "P." She laughs and we laugh and she keeps laughing and then, in one elegant motion, she steps off the desk. And I swear she floats slowly to the floor, her bare feet landing without a sound (or maybe I can't hear it amidst all the laughter).

She walks past me to the windows. I turn to follow just as the students rise from their desks and follow as well, they leave their notebooks and textbooks behind and follow, just as I leave my lecture notes behind and follow. The woman holds out her hands and the outside wall of the Clearihue Building is no longer there, you can see it but somehow it doesn't matter, and she leads us outside.

Outside we can see everything, the library next door, the fountain, the entire city laid out beyond the trees, everything as solid and transparent as the Clearihue wall. There is a spark of sunlight on every surface, in every window.

We are three storeys up, three storeys in the air, but it doesn't matter. When we're ready we simply float to the ground. We land, weightless, and there are other people there, students and staff and faculty, some of whom have places to go and look at their feet but others who watch us with wide open eyes. Next thing everyone dances off in his or her own direction, and some are already taking off their clothes, and the young woman is everywhere and nowhere to be found. And I hope that when they arrive wherever they are going, my students will tell their family or lovers or friends, or maybe even a perfect stranger, that in English 453 this term we really did learn how to practice freedom.

# WHY I WAS TEN MINUTES LATE GETTING HOME

I got back to my office after
lunch with Al Purdy and Eurithe
and it was only quarter past three
lots of time to pack up and ride
home by four (as agreed) except
there was a student camped outside
my door with that look students
give you when the sign on your door
says you'll be back by two-thirty
and it's quarter past three
She came inside sat in
the chair we rescued from
the garbage on St. Clair West
(remember our apartment back then
the store below with the magical
name of "Ideal Yarns") said she
was having trouble with
her essay on *The Diviners*
"I want to write on gender issues"
she explained and I replied
"could you be more specific?"
For ten minutes we tried to be
more specific and I gave her
a book about writing essays
I was about to close the door
when a woman stuck in her head
a book rep from Toronto
here for one day only
did I have a minute?

She showed me a new anthology
for first year English and I explained
I rarely teach first year anymore
(unfortunately) at which point we
fell into quite a pleasant
discussion of mystery novels

From here things get complicated
beginning with how I noticed it
was twenty to four
and said I had to go
I grabbed my stuff and
rushed down the hall only
to realize I'd forgotten
the copy of *Piling Blood* I bought
from Eurithe at the reading
I was aching to get at it and
figured it would only take
a sec to run back
and it did except that
when I finally got downstairs
and made to unlock my bike
I realized my keys were
back on my desk

And so on

I know you don't want to hear
the entire saga of the keys
how they weren't on my desk
and how I ended up apologizing
to the room full of
Japanese exchange students
but at least let me
tell you about the branch
that tangled my gears
how my chain kept slipping off
let me tell you about the
rain and gale force winds

What I'm trying to
say really I guess or at least
what I've been circling around
all this time is that it had to do
with Purdy—Al Purdy and the beers
we drank before and during
and after lunch (while Eurithe
sipped tea) the stories we told
the gossip and the stuff
between the lines
Goddamn poets and goddamn poetry
with their promises of a deeper life
getting me drunk and
confused with yearning in
the middle of the afternoon

# ARSE POETICA

## ARSE POETICA

To avoid
incarceration within, a prison.

In the first place, the elaborated
and "logical."

The great master of metaphor
seems to be presented to us always in the ironic.

Logic is nearly always
in the pool of water, warped and bent.

What is true of the poet's language
is true.

But the proof is
not proof.

(Using logic so that the best of his poems
are not fumbling and loose.)

The task:
to "dislocate language into."

# IDLE TEARS

In the second place, where
"Tears, Idle Tears"
will scarcely prove to the hard-boiled

the relation between term and meaning.
It is the child
who is the best philosopher.

Pressures exerted by various symbols
in this poem "prove" an essentially
illogical one.

There is a profound irony forced
to remake language.
This general sense, then, is to be found.

We have, of course, been taught to
consider the statement immersed in
a kind of darkness. To overthrow

interest, a pair of compasses.
The ideal language would contain
one term.

# "WE OUGHT NOT TO BE SURPRISED IF THE STATE"

We ought not to be surprised if the state
uses "logic," regularly uses
it to justify illogi-telescoped
figures like "Made of the images in

Shakespeare's sonnets." Conventional crit
has been heretofore fined in advance. They
are not to be warped into new as an
extrication from, but as "shadowy"—

that the light proceeds. As to why this must
be, there is irony of a very
powerful sort in not to say certainly.
Not avoided by the poet: they are.

Indeed, the great show of logic; but two
figures must prove even his staple one.

# THE DEVIL EVEN THIS

The devil is not life at
all. He is simply trying

to spice up, to assert that
myth is truer fact, to possess

the world. In his own experience,
the symbol is father to

the man, the dawn light is
still, as part from part, lovers

are really saints with fire. Wishes
must express a life which is

above life and its vicissitudes, but
all of us are familiar with

the censure, a kind of death.
To put it in other terms:

ambiguity and paradox
rather than plain,

in the hopes that the fires
be content with saying even this.

# Here Again The Evening Light

Here again his own experience.
To adopt multiple vision, the
poet must prove that a
poem parts, just as any
mere statement itself. For even
this poem, which testifies so
heavily, typifies less spectacularly than
the saint. At least, it
is an "imitation"—necessarily, world.
Discursive seems both
dead and alive, also accounts
for the dogmatic light. Vision
has been above life and
the thoroughness of the world.
Life is not life at
all (the drama of the
structure). The hope of content:
the common symbol to indicate
even after the worst. "Father."
From a matter of paying
tribute, then dramatization in
a paradox lovers must reject.
A kind of death. A
great many of us still
are rhetorical, split up, historian,
giving up the world, the
union of opposites, the same
light as the evening light.

## Sonny Talks To Me From Beyond Grave

1.

In which he claims he has proof of the experience,
the rain, a tree, a hotline.

Heaven seems both dead and alive.

He left her house but the creaks continue to
love her.

She is fighting the devil, memory, the host of
Sonny & Me, the unity of the experience.

To put it in other terms, "Chat, chat, chat."

She wanted to know the last thing, touching tearful
words about him, where the dictionary was, the
root-black fingers.

"I'll always be there for you."

2.

I have a bond that's close to Sonny, his task
to unify experience, tour Larry King Live, the
human world.

Not to mention his book.

They christen him All-Ball, stubborn as hell,
"meaning" and visual splendour.

We carry on a dramatic conversation, present
consciousness and the translucid perception of
present qualities.

"Put soul into this special," says a source.

Heaven is nodes of memory.

In the bedroom, we postpone the act, put off
perception, give over the years, tears, clean or
boiled water, context, exact orders.

"Sonny kept laughing, he was both dead and alive,
he mentioned Koko looking out, a CBS TV special,
a poem."

Death hosts the TV special, vibrant as vocal cords.

3.

Sonny also mentioned personal details, the swings
in the park, painted benches, small combs, slippers,
toothbrushes, irony, signals across the boundaries
of structures, the sky filling up with satellites,
faces over shirts and ties, Donne's lovers, the
force of memory, spices, the mouth, the unknown
fold, the number 8, missile size, the "nitty-gritty,"
our terrible labour, a better world.

He lived his whole life loving her.

"The main thing that I remember is inner maps,
released from the constraints."

To pull the boat outward, provisioned with burdens,
amends, colours, the ability to distinguish had
and will.

The sheet of ice, boundless.

Sonny also talked about things which govern the
whole of Freud's thought and determine the ways
in which the spirits come to you.

So that what we have are humans, who never die,
who are determined outside any teleological or
eschatological horizon.

Which is not and is serene, a waking sleep.

"Somehow the same light as the evening light," says
a pal.

4.

After death we can't spit out ourselves.

After the split, the "effect of deferral," the
cities with paper, whole stores, a woman standing
angry.

I was skeptical.

"What is to come of muscle, tendon, cartilage,
bone, serum, members, the CBS TV special, exquisite
marks, the problem of oral and written, the cholera
epidemic in Peru, pack ice, poison?"

There are over 500 words for Fame.

The body tells STAR: "I felt."

It seems plausible, a potential, a nexus.

Death, that repetition beyond the pleasure
principle, native, a bond that's close to Sonny,
like the swings in the park, squeak, squeak,
like the scratch at the back of the brain.

The same principle that inspires the presence of
the sheet of ice, the last thing, the telephone
(which wouldn't work for no apparent reason).

"I'm not dead," Sonny told her, "pull that across
the ice with your tendonous body."

A door high up in a tree.

5.

In which he claims he has proof, meaning contiguous
with the bodies' motion, the famed medium, a cure for
cholera.

Larry King, Oprah, Descartes, Marx.

Our hands coming up, almost.

When we consider the statement, dressed casually in
jeans and a loose shirt, Koko the talking gorilla,
analytic reason, long black hair flowing behind.

Who says it's all a trick—Polly, Polly?

He recalls that she was desperate for answers, her
hands muscular, the excess of being.

She is so heartbroken.

Let us not hasten to define this other of pure
quantity, an electrical passage, the discovery of
ultimate consequences.

"Are you an animal or a person?"

6.

He said that was him, inner meaning jettisoned
outside the body.

Thanks a lot for being.

In an exclusive interview, he told how he helped a
tailless kitten, millions of Americans, the great
master of metaphor.

"Yeah, that's the way he was in real life."

To put it in other terms, a Malibu home, the
history of water, chat, chat, chat, and "She was
a believer."

She cried and she laughed.

She wanted it to be perfect.

The rigor of it and the thoroughness of it, the
swings in the park, young children convincing even
the most dogmatic.

*7.*

To adopt a metaphor, "a pair of heels to
match death."

He said that "The body itself is the hieroglyph"
and mentioned how nice the funeral had been, the
economy of death, deferment, repetition, reserve.

She cried and she laughed.

"I remember Denver, Cordoba, Rome, The Saint,
electrical currents in the house, an original
plenitude."

"It is a non-origin which is originary," Sonny said.

8.

In the pack ice, a door left hanging, an
abandoned tradition, the "history of water,"
a very tenuous concept.

Unsolved Mysteries.

The spirit is a categorization, a motion in
the head awakened under the compulsion of
the exigencies of life.

And now she wants to make amends.

The hungry choose, in a dream.

Love can conquer Oslo, Leningrad, Peking,
Thunder Bay.

Your hand on mine, pulling us upward, what we no
longer recognize as memory.

The unity of the experience.

"Nothing will ever break it," she told pals.

AFTERWARD

The poems in "Arse Poetica" were generated using various collage techniques. All of shorter poems were generated from pages 220-23 of Cleanth Brooks's famous essay "The Heresy of Paraphrase" in *The Well Wrought Urn* (1947).

"Sonny Talks to Me From Beyond Grave" was generated from the same pages in Brooks and the following:

Pearson, Jennifer and Beverly Williston. "Cher: Sonny Talks to Me From Beyond Grave." *Star* (May 19, 1998): 24-5.

Wallace, Bronwen. "Koko." *Stubborn Particulars of Grace*. Toronto: M & S, 1987. 85-7.

Mouré, Erin. "Speed, or Absolute Structure." *Sheepish Beauty, Civilian Love*. Montreal: Véhicule, 1992. 40-5.

Derrida, Jacques. "Freud and the Scene of Writing." *Writing and Difference*. Trans. Alan Bass. Chicago: U of Chicago P, 1978. 202-3 (only).